Marine Archaeology

Other titles in this series:

Cassell's Introducing Archaeology Series

Marine Archaeology

ELISHA LINDER and AVNER RABAN

Cassell · London

CASSELL & COMPANY LTD
Cassell & Collier Macmillan Publishers Ltd
35 Red Lion Square, London WCIR 4SG
and at Sydney, Auckland, Toronto, Johannesburg
and an affiliate of The Macmillan Company Inc,
New York

913.031 Elisha
Lindey

Designed by Ofra Kamar

First published in Great Britain 1975

I.S.B.N. 0 304 29337 7

Printed by Peli Press, Ltd., Givatayim.

PRINTED IN ISRAEL

F. 1274

main Line - 9-12-77 - 14.98 - quals
space

INTRODUCTION

The study of seafaring in antiquity has reached a turning-point with the development of underwater archaeology. A well defined scientific discipline has emerged, based on the chance finds of ancient artefacts hauled up from the sea bottom. This discipline is concerned with the problems of shipbuilding and navigation; with the construction and use of harbour installations; and with the archaeological research of coastal cities, parts of which are still submerged. As a result of the use of proper tools and techniques for excavation and the adoption of systematic methods for recording information, underwater archaeology has become the legitimate offspring of land archaeology, its scientific validity acknowledged by even the most sceptical and conservative scholars.

However, as often occurs, the benefits extend even beyond the field of research for which specific tools are developed. New fields of interest with different emphasis and direction are opened up, thus widening our scope of knowledge. Once the techniques enabling the exploration and excavation of shipwrecks and submerged structures were mastered, historians became more aware of the important role played by the sea in the growth of various civilizations. Therefore, we may call this new discipline "marine archaeology", encompassing as it does the whole complex of man's past involvement with maritime trade and communication, naval warfare, coastal industry and economy, and cultural inter-relation between distant centres of civilization. Our emphasis is thus placed on the sea itself, though we are well aware of the impact of lakes and rivers upon the development of boats and water transport.

The major part of this book is devoted to the Mediterranean, since the earliest history of seafaring is linked to this sea. On the bed of the Mediterranean we find abundant evidence of maritime activity going back for more than ten thousand years. Furthermore, the growing number of publications on marine archaeology indicate that the eastern Mediterranean in particular is less familiar to the reader,

Above: Hellenistic wreck on reef at Yassi-Ada   *Right:* Wreck of Austrian brig at Porto Longo

Diver recovering Phoenician amphora from bed of Old Harbour at Atlit

be he layman or professional. In the past decade substantial research has been undertaken in both the Mediterranean and the Red Sea, adding new dimensions to our knowledge of shipping in these waters — a subject of great interest to anyone concerned with ancient Near Eastern history.

I THE BEGINNINGS

What may be called the first underwater archaeological venture took place in 1446, when a group of Genoese divers attempted to recover two Roman ships sunk in Lake Nemi near Rome. Nearly five hundred years later, divers equipped with modern apparatus carried out the excavation of an ancient wreck discovered near Albenga in Italy. This event marked the beginning of the new discipline of marine archaeology.

Then, with the accidental discovery of extraordinary works of art at the bottom of the Mediterranean, archaeologists began to realize the significance of the sea in the study of ancient civilizations. This came about at the beginning of the century, off the coast of Antikythera. A Greek sponge diver surfaced from a depth of 30 fathoms shouting excitedly: "Horses... naked women... people... a city". He had just discovered a wreck from the 1st century BC, loaded with bronzes and marble works of art. The salvage operation that followed, under the supervision of the Greek authorities, yielded among other sculptures one of the finest bronzes ever discovered, now known as the "Youth of Antikythera".

Several years later, in 1907, came the discovery of the Mahdia wreck off the coast of Tunisia. Again it was Greek sponge divers who found it; they discovered a large number of marble columns and blocks from which protruded parts of life-size statues.

In 1928, two masterpieces of Greek sculpture dating to the 5th century BC were found by divers at Cape Artemision, off the Greek island of Euboea. These, a Zeus and a jockey with part of a galloping horse, are only samples from a cargo which still lies at the bottom of the sea awaiting further exploration. Nearly half a century later, two of the sites were revisited and their finds reexamined. This time, with the use of new methods of scientific underwater exploration, the difference in approach became apparent. The ancient artefacts found were no longer considered to be merely museum pieces with very little relation to the entire complex of the ship and its cargo. Now, an attempt was

The bronze boy

ever, the methods employed to excavate this site, and particularly those used to recover the ship's cargo, now seem entirely obsolete. To the marine archaeologist, the idea of using a grab operating from a salvage vessel is as appalling as the thought of using a bulldozer to excavate an ancient site would be to the land archaeologist.

A step forward was taken two years later when a French team headed by Commander Jacques-Yves Cousteau and Frédéric Dumas undertook the exploration of a Roman wreck from the 2nd century BC, dicovered by an amateur diver at Grand Congloué, near the port of Marseilles. Here, for the first time, proper tools for the retrieval and re-recording of artefacts were developed. An "Air-Lift" was developed to serve as an exposing tool and underwater photography was introduced.

This expedition did not achieve perfection, neither was its recording of finds archaeologically sound. A number of basic problems regarding the site of the wreck were left open to dispute. None the less, the large Roman merchant ship yielded a wealth of information concerning the wine trade in the 2nd century BC, and assisted the classification of various kinds of pottery.

The lessons learned from the Grand Congloué excavation influenced the work of Commander Philippe Taillez

made to study each site as a whole, by piecing together all the evidence recovered.

The excavation of a wreck discovered near Albenga in 1950 was the first attempt to introduce a systematic method of marine archaeological exploration, as opposed to the salvage of ships. How-

during his investigation of the *Titan* wreck in 1958, discovered by chance off the eastern point of the Île du Levant, off the Côte d'Azur. Here, for the first time, a stratigraphic excavation was attempted, followed by the immediate recording of all artefacts *in situ*. Their exact position was measured to a marked "base-line"; a method which has become regular procedure in underwater exploration. Furthermore, each stage of excavation was photographed. The work was so meticulously executed that, besides the amphoras and other types of pottery, even the smallest objects, such as coins or almonds, were detected and recorded.

While the French were toiling away on the wreck of the *Titan,* an Italian team headed by Prof. N. Lamboglia was excavating a Roman merchant ship discovered between Sardinia and the island of Spargi, at a depth of 18 metres. Evidently, the "inferior" excavation methods used on the Albenga wreck, and the resultant damage to ship and cargo, inspired the meticulous excavation of the Spargi wreck. The use of a grid for exact mapping purposes, together with photomosaic documentation, were innovations which soon became standard for every systematic wreck investigation.

These have been some of the stages in the development of marine archaeology,

How the amphorae had been stacked in the Grand Congloué wreck

arising from the accidental discovery of wrecks and the subsequent excavation of the ships and their cargoes. The next phase in this area of scientific research begins with the deliberate search for, and planned exploration of, harbours and submerged land sites. These investigations will be discussed in later chapters.

II THE INNER SPACE

Readers who are interested in the result — the "find" — are sure to want to know the story behind its discovery, both the physical background and the human part of the story. Let us therefore take a close look at the element which protects the secrets, the sea—that three-dimensional expanse which covers three-quarters of the earth, and upon whose constantly moving and stormy surface our forefathers sailed to establish settlements and to trade with unknown worlds. Our intention is not to deal with the wide field of oceanography but rather to concentrate on more basic concepts. In so doing, we shall acquaint the reader more intimately with one of the world's most intriguing seas, the Mediterranean. Although this sea is not much larger in area than the Great Lakes, the Hudson Bay or the Gulf of Mexico, it more than makes up for its size in other ways.

1. *The Mediterranean – Cradle of Sea-faring*

The basic ideas of western civilization were born along the shores of the Medi-terranean Sea. Across this body of water the earliest Egyptian Pharaohs made contact with cultures outside the Nile Valley; it was traversed by the armies of the Persians and the Medes in order to conquer Europe; the armies of Macedonia and Rome travelled across it in opposite directions to shape the civilized world of their day into a *Koine* – a single cultural unit. The Mediterranean was crossed from west to east by the heavily armoured Crusaders, bound to free the Holy Land from the infidels, aboard the ships of the Italian city states of Venice, Genoa and Pisa. These same Crusaders often turned to trade, taking home rare goods and natural resources formerly unknown in the cities of Europe.

In the centuries that followed, the Mediterranean was "closed" to Europeans by the navies of the Turkish rulers and the Barbary Coast pirate ships of Algeria and Morocco. This take-over induced daring Portuguese and Spanish seamen to search for alternative trade-routes to the East; it led them to the discovery of a sea route to India around the shores of Africa; and to the discovery of the great continents of the Western Hemisphere.

But the discovery of alternative sailing routes did not for long diminish the importance of the Mediterranean. When the rush to conquer unclaimed lands in the New World slowed down, the Mediterranean once again became the scene of international imperialistic and economic rivalry. And thus, in the last century, this sea was witness to the race between the forces of Britain and France and to the intrigues of their statesmen for control of its eastern (Suez Canal) and western (Gibraltar) gates.

This is the Mediterranean: the arena of historical events, and the area connecting — or dividing — the cultures which have matured along its shores. The exchange of goods and the transfer of raw materials have taken place across its waters and with them the exchange of technological knowledge, improvements, and inventions. This sea has provided inestimable wealth for those who control its trade routes, and has driven them to develop the ability and instruments to navigate at night (celestial navigation) and on to the high seas.

The Mediterranean is an "inland" sea, connecting Africa, Europe and Asia. It penetrates deep into the east, where it joins with the Black Sea (by way of the Dardanelles and Bosphorus) and the Red Sea and Indian Ocean (over the land straits of Suez and southern Israel).

There are no strong currents in the Mediterranean and the movement of the water is mainly due to an off-shore wind which sweeps down from the mountains to the sea. Its basin is not subject to sudden wind changes. For most of the year there is a constant flow of air from the north-east. Even when stormy conditions prevail the waves do not rise above 8 metres, about half the height of the highest waves of the Atlantic. It is a deep sea, averaging 1,500 metres and reaching a depth of 4,600 metres in the strait between Greece and Crete, with a very narrow continental shelf, except for the shallow Adriatic Sea.

2. Geophysical Changes in the Mediterranean

One of the important physical properties for the marine archaeologist is the geological instability of the Mediterranean: that is, 'eustatic' sea-level changes and tectonic movements along the coastline.

The term "eustatic changes" means world-wide changes caused by a variation in the amount of water trapped in the ice-caps at the poles subtracted from the amount of water in the oceans and semi-inland seas linked to them.

This phenomenon has been subject to continuous study, employing various approaches; here are two examples.

An Israeli chemist, Dr M. Bloch of the Negev Institute for Arid Zone Research, has been studying the effect of eustatic changes in the sea level on the economies of coastal plains settlements which become flooded with every minor change in the level of the sea. The basis of Dr Bloch's research is the importance of salt and its major sources of mining and production in the economy of mankind. In order to reconstruct a reliable and fairly accurate picture of such eustatic changes, Dr. Bloch collected historical data, especially from western and northern Europe, on the price-fluctuations of this commodity; contemporary reports on the abandoning of *salinas* (evaporation pools for the production of salt); data on the drying-up of ports and the opening up of new salt fields (with the fall in sea level). Furthermore, Dr Bloch continued to look for the impact of the changing geophysical background on the geopolitical processes by studying the effect of the changes in sea level on a society whose economy is dependent upon the sea.

Dr N. C. Flemming, oceanographer and geologist, of the Royal Oceanographic Institute in Surrey, believes that the local tectonic changes — particularly in the eastern Mediterranean — are of greater importance than the world-wide eustatic changes. Drawing on the basic premise that the direction and rate of movement have not changed significantly in the last 3,000 years, Dr Flemming has gathered archaeological data from coastal settlements and ancient harbours along the coast of Greece, and the Aegean Islands, Crete and the western coast of Asia Minor. His work was carried out in an attempt to determine the relation of the architectural structures to the seas by defining their function, and thus determining the past and present sea level. Correlation of the data for all these settlements permits the reconstruction of a tectonic map encompassing the major part of the central and northern Mediterranean. If we accept it as being correct, this map helps us understand historical and geopolitical events (the rise and fall of port cities and "maritime" kingdoms) and gives an indication of where to look for remains of maritime structures submerged in deep water, adjusted to the present-day sea level or covered by silt on land.

3. *Down to the Sea*

In the following chapters we describe what the sea has revealed to us up to now. In the rest of this chapter we shall consider what one can expect to discover in the sea or retrieve from it — not necessarily in terms of a random find of this or that wreck, but within a system-

Aerial photograph (1943) of Trajanic harbour at Ostia, in use today as water reservoir

atic framework of orderly research, with work techniques and reliable, tested methods developed specifically for this type of investigation. Let us then go down to the sea and see what awaits us and what is demanded of us in overcoming the obstacles placed in our path. Let us not forget, at the same time, that these very obstacles have preserved the remnants of the past until this very day. Had they been on land, they would have been lost to science and mankind many generations ago.

In the sea we can expect to find the remains both of maritime activity and of coastal activity — including entire settlements — which geophysical changes caused to sink below sea level. Of course, there is a great difference between these two types of find. With regard to finds on land, methods and techniques similar to those used in conventional archaeology must be used. The careful search for the answer to the central question must be sought: what is the chronological relationship between the time of settlement (or human activity on land) and the time of submergence? How much time elapsed between the two events, and how much has elapsed between the submergence and today? With regard to maritime activity the picture is clearer. On a specific date a certain unique event occurred — a disaster — in which a ship sank, or ran aground, or was caught in a storm, or, as a result of some disaster, its frightened crew tossed cargo or equipment overboard in order to lighten the load and thereby escape being wrecked.

To these two types of find a third, marginal, one may be added — finds which have been carried along by flooding rivers or coastal currents (especially rip currents) from land near by to the sea bed. But these are haphazard finds, usually found out of context, and therefore they cannot be used for scientific purposes.

4. *How the Sea Conceals and Preserves*

The sea treats the objects sunk in its depths in different ways — depending on the prevailing geophysical conditions. Those submerged in shallow water are ground and smashed by waves whose force is felt to a depth of more than five times their height. What has sunk on a rocky or pebbly sea bed is open to the compound destruction of currents and movement of the water (erosion) and of marine plants and animals. On the other hand, what has sunk on a deep sea bed of silt or mud is covered mainly by a layer of that deposit and is completely preserved beneath it. In this case, we may expect to find items made of perishable material which would not survive on land for very long, certainly not more

Small objects recovered from the muddy sea bottom near Haifa

than a few generations. However, in underwater conditions where there is a lack of oxygen, the process of degeneration or rust is retarded, and these items are found in a relatively good state of preservation.

These include wooden parts of shipwrecks, anchors, copper and iron nails, and cargoes consisting mainly of pottery and even of organic materials like reeds, skins, or cloth. True, we do not expect to find the ship in the condition in which it sank. Its own weight and that of its cargo gradually flattens the ship's sides

outwards and it sprawls on the bottom of the sea, covered by a layer of sand and mud which protects it from biogenic destruction.

In another type of sea bed, a rocky one, we expect that in the absence of protective sediments the wooden parts and other perishable materials will be found in an advanced state of decomposition or be absent altogether, except for some objects buried under the cargo. Articles made of metal (especially iron) would be subject to oxidation (much slower than on land but often fast

Above: Terra cottafigurine recovered from the sea, encrusted with marine fauna
Right: A figurine after cleaning

enough to disintegrate the metal completely) and, at the same time, of encrustation, either biological or mineral. We often find a shapeless chalky block in which is preserved a hollow "negative" of an iron nail, the blade of an axe, the barrel of a rifle, or a sword, which has since disintegrated. Thus, for example, several very heavily encrusted Crusader swords were found near Caesarea. Although the general shapes of swords could be identified, X-ray pictures were necessary in order to recognize their original form and details.

Regarding the various degrees of preservation we find a great difference between the north-western Mediterranean and its south-eastern regions, or the Red Sea. While in the relatively cold and clear water of the north the processes of disintegration and encrustation are comparatively slow, in the south and east the warm waters result in an increased activity of marine life, hastening the processes. In the Red Sea, artefacts found as deep as 30 to 40 metres form a base for the speedy growth of coral reefs. In one case, a large wreck 300 years old was covered with a coral "forest" over one metre thick! In order to recover the

Globular jar covered with corals, on the bed of the Red Sea

finds, it is actually necessary to dig through the reef with pneumatic drills.

In shallow water, the chances of preservation are greatly reduced. Only a rare combination of circumstances such as a soft, muddy sea bed and the immediate covering of the wreck with a protective layer of sediments will preserve the artefacts.

III TOOLS AND TECHNIQUES

For the past decade, the historical study of the Holy Land has been furthered by the organization of a methodical archaeological survey. The area under survey is thoroughly examined and the material evidence for human activity throughout the ages is recorded in detail. When compared to such an extensive land survey, a similar project at sea is far more difficult.

1. *Problems of Underwater Survey*

On land, the archaeologist can spot an artefact from a distance, so that his rate of progress is about three kilometres per hour; work can be carried out for five or six hours a day. At sea, however, when a diver is surveying the sea bed in a muddy area of the eastern Mediterranean at a depth of 25 or 30 metres, his visibility is limited to one or two metres in every direction. The diver can stay underwater no more than two hours a day, and his rate of progress is less than one kilometre per hour; thus 150 to 200 diving days would be required to complete a survey of one square kilometre of sea bed! If we consider that conditions at sea permit this type of activity for only one-third of the year, and if we add the need for a great deal of expensive equipment such as boats, diving apparatus, compressors, surveyors' instruments and a complex set of ropes and buoys, the challenge becomes even greater. Fortunately, tools for the job are constantly being developed, thanks to the growing interest of the world in the natural resources of the sea and the urgent need to conquer the "inner space". Archaeological relics scattered over the bottom of the sea serve as an ideal "model" for testing and improvement of such equipment. This allows for the rapid development of sophisticated equipment originally meant for economic purposes but used with success by marine archaeology. Let us elaborate upon a number of tools and instruments which have been developed recently and their application to marine archaeological search, identification and retrieval methods.

2. *Towing the Diver*

With this method, the survey is carried out by a boat towing a diver through the water. The diver holds on to a wooden board by two handles; by moving these he can change the angle of the board, to determine his height above the sea bed, according to visibility, the nature of the sea bottom, the depth of the water, and the speed at which he is being towed. The navigator of the boat uses a set of buoys to make sure that the area under survey is thoroughly covered. Every time a suspicious-looking object is spotted on the sea bed, the diver inspects and marks it. For efficiency and safety the boat usually tows from two to four divers in a close frontal line. If the diver is well trained and uses a diving mask and snorkel of a type which cannot be swept away by the pressure of the counter-current, the survey can be carried out up to three times as fast as by normal diving procedure.

A more advanced piece of equipment is a hydrodynamic cradle. The diver lies on a metal "bed" (usually of aluminium), protected by a perspex "window", while his hands manipulate hydrodynamic elevation handles on either side of the cradle to control his distance from the bottom. A special installation enables the diver, by pulling a lever, to release a marker buoy when he spots a suspected find without having to interrupt the search. Later, the find can be examined more closely by the team. The improved cradles in use today are equipped with a communications system which permits conversation between the diver in the cradle and the navigator of the boat. This method requires training and experience to keep the cradle properly balanced and steered, as well as a trained eye for the quick identification of artefacts on the sea bottom. Such a cradle can be towed at a speed of 3 knots, thus enabling the diver to cover relatively large areas within a short time.

3. *The Towvane*

An additional improvement in underwater towing is the towvane. This is a bell-shaped metal container designed to hold one or two divers who stand inside and survey the sea bed through plexiglass windows. The towvane can be used either as a towed closed submarine or as a diving-bell. In the second and preferable method, a section of the floor is cut out so the divers can leave the enclosure easily while hooking on to the breathing apparatus on their backs. The towvane also requires hydrodynamic steering with elevation boards manipulated by the divers, and it includes a telephone communications system connected to the towing boat. It is a so-

Above: Recording under water
Below: Diver surveying with the "cradle"
Left: Preliminaries to recording on the sea bed

The Towvane at work

phisticated device, expensive and some-what complicated, and its efficiency is dependent on good visibility — at least 5 to 6 metres in each direction near the sea bottom. Finds are marked with a buoy released from inside the towvane.

4. *The Cubmarine*

The most advanced method of underwater survey, still using the eyes of the skilled diver, is the small submarine nicknamed the "cubmarine". There are a number of models being developed and several already in use. The simplest of these are capable of reaching a depth of 50 to 60 metres and are operated by a pair of divers. They are powered by

electrical batteries and are navigated by "rudders", or water jets. A more advanced model can be equipped with claws or arms which pick up samples; a strong lighting system to overcome problems of visibility; and stereoscopic cameras. The *Ashera,* the research submarine originally owned by the University of Pennsylvania Museum, is of this type. With it, a crew under Professor G. F. Bass managed to discover a sunken cargo along the coast of Turkey and map it three-dimensionally by the use of stereoscopic photography in less than one hour at a depth of 40 metres and more. The most advanced type of submarine was recently developed by the well-known American inventor Edwin

Link; it has two compartments, one for the navigator and scientist, and the other for two divers who can enter and leave the submarine while underwater.

5. *Sonar Replaces the Human Eye*

The problem of surveying the sea bed can be approached from another angle. There remain difficulties and limitations when using divers' physical fitness, underwater skills, and the ability to distinguish "man-made objects" even when their form has been blurred or twisted by marine encrustation.* However, the examination of archaeological relics covered by sea growth or layers of sand or mud which cannot be detected by the naked eye necessitates the development of other techniques — the use of electronic instruments operated from the surface.

The sea bed can be searched by means of a conventional echo-sounder. This is an instrument now used in almost every ship; it determines the depth of the sea directly below, by sending out a sound wave and calculating the time it takes to receive an echo from the bottom. The echo-sounder not only marks on a graph the changing depth of the sea below the moving boat, but with a little experience,

---

* These can be overcome by intensive training and extensive experience on the part of the diver.

one can determine the type of sea bed by reading the quality and clarity of the recorded graph. This technique has been developed in particular by Prof. H. Edgerton of the Massachusetts Institute of Technology who built the "pinger" and the "mud penetrator". Both instruments are based on the principle of low frequency sound waves which can penetrate and differentiate between the densities of various materials.

Such sonar instruments were used successfully in archaeological research for the first time in 1963, at the Herodian harbour of Caesarea. There, beneath the sandy sea bottom, the remains of several harbour installations were disclosed. Sonar was also instrumental in locating the *Mary Rose* off the coast near Portsmouth, as well as wrecks and submerged structures in the Peloponnese and in the Red Sea.

The main drawback of the penetrating sonar method is the narrow path it surveys. This means that the route must be carefully planned to ensure complete coverage of the area under survey. In the open sea, this requires the use of highly complex navigation systems, including buoys and location markers. Another drawback is the need to put out a marker buoy the instant something suspicious appears on the record.

A significant improvement is marked by the development of the side-scan sonar. Differing from its predecessor, which operates on the principle of vertical sound waves, this instrument can receive a diagonal returning echo. This makes it possible to get a picture of the sea bed at a distance of 100 to 300 metres right and/or left of the route plied by the boat. The side-scan sonar enables one to "see" a wide strip of the sea bed independent of unfavourable visibility conditions at the time of the survey. In order to ensure good results it is necessary for the crew using the side-scan sonar to practise its operation with well-trained divers and to set up a navigational system based on shore stations.

6. *Underwater Television*

Another device which has had considerable success in the islands of the Aegean Sea and in the western Mediterranean is the television camera, towed underwater. A complex system of lights and closed circuit television cameras is towed at a set level and angle above the sea bed; these can be controlled, monitored, and watched on board the towing boat.

The method's major drawback is that its efficiency is dependent upon the clarity of the water, the calmness of the sea, and on the perfect working order of the remote control system.

7. *The Metal Detector*

There are two instruments designed for detecting metal, one of which is the proton magnetometer developed by Dr T. Hall of Oxford University, England. Its active part, the sensor, is towed a substantial distance behind the boat and is connected to it by a watertight and insulated line. In 1966 at the archaeological expedition in Acre harbour, the device proved itself capable of locating iron objects whose mass was not more than a few kilogrammes at a distance of 100 or even 200 metres. Generally, the instrument will give us a provisional estimate of the size of the object located. While the proton magnometer is expensive and elaborate in its operation, another simpler instrument is the metal detector reacting primarily to metal objects and operated by a diver and his assistant.

————————

We opened this chapter with a description of the Mediterranean Sea and have concluded with an account of sophisticated instruments designed to help unlock its secrets. However, the use of expensive and complicated instruments cannot take the place of the experienced diver whose senses are developed to the point where he can spot artefacts on the bottom of the sea

Diver in underwater survey

which are almost indistinguishable from the natural phenomena.

The following is a good illustration. The Crusader castle of Atlit is situated on a promontory south of Haifa. For years its northern bay served as an active diving ground while providing an extremely interesting underwater landscape with its abundance of fish and natural formations. Only after years of training and experience in underwater archaeological excavations did it become clear that all those "rocks" and "reefs" in the Atlit bay were man-made; parts of jetties, moles and piers which made up the plan of an artificially built harbour.

a) THE MEDITERRANEAN

After ten years of excavating sunken wrecks in the Mediterranean, it became clear to archaeologists that they would have to join forces with professional divers to introduce a systematic search for further ancient wrecks. Differences in cultural backgrounds and mentality, as well as language barriers, made such collaboration between the sophisticated scientist and the simple fisherman or amateur diver a very difficult task. However, the link was established by an amateur diver-archaeologist.

Peter Throckmorton, American journalist-photographer, seaman and diver, by following his innate feeling for exploration and interest in archaeology, obtained some of the most important information on ancient wreck sites along the Turkish and Greek coasts. He joined a team of Turkish sponge divers, shared their bread and hardships for over a year, learned their language, listened to their stories, gained their confidence, and was initiated into their intimate knowledge of the sea-bottom. While diving with his new friends, he discovered scores of wreck sites which he meticulously recorded, plotting their positions so that he was later able to return and develop his study.

1. Cape Gelidonya

In 1960, Throckmorton presented this wealth of information to Professor George Bass, a classical archaeologist at the Pennsylvania University Museum. After visiting many of the sites discovered by Throckmorton, Bass chose a wreck site at Cape Gelidonya near Bodrum, Turkey. Here on the sea bottom lay a Canaanite ship from the 12th century BC which had carried a cargo of copper ingots and bronze utensils, and had a coppersmith's workshop on board. Up to then it was the oldest wreck ever discovered, and it served to unlock the previously unknown story of seafaring 3000 years ago.

Bass had no difficulty in gathering together an enthusiastic group of experts

Measuring a copper ingot in the Cape Gelidonya wreck

from the United States, England, France and other countries. Several major achievements can be attributed to the Gelidonya wreck excavation: methods and techniques were developed and standard procedure in land excavation was successfully adapted by Bass. Working at a depth of 30 metres, he had to cope with physiological problems of deep diving, heavy currents and other natural obstacles. Nevertheless, finds were precisely recorded, objects which were heavily concreted were removed from the sea bottom with minimum damage, wood and metal artefacts were reconstructed and preserved very satisfactorily. Every member of the team contributed his share, and several of them later became independent marine archaeologists in their right. Thus, Frédéric Dumas, who collaborated with Cousteau in the development of the aqualung, developed specific techniques for underwater survey and excavation which became part of the groundwork for underwater archaeology. His superb mastery of diving and of underwater work dispensed with the then existing doubts that an archaeologist could work effectively in that medium once so hostile to researchers.

Another example is Honor Frost, who began her marine archaeological career with Bass as a draftsman-artist, later successfully developed a method of dating and classifying stone anchors, and has recently specialized in employing aerial photography for three-dimensional mapping of submerged structures.

Bass became involved in a project which proved a turning-point in his personal career, and influenced the professional future of those pioneers who joined him.

Returning to the Gelidonya wreck, the analysis of its cargo of copper and bronze ingots, bronze tools and weapons led to a re-evaluation of our knowledge of the copper trade in the late Bronze Age. No less important are the historical inferences drawn by Bass. On sound archaeological evidence, he deduced from the finds (which included pottery, scarabs, weights, cylinder seals, etc.) that Syro-Phoenician traders dominated the eastern Mediterranean enterprises, thus challenging the generally accepted view of Mycenaean hegemony of the seas at that period.

2. *Yassi Ada*

The Byzantine wreck excavated near the Turkish island of Yassi Ada in the S.E. Aegean* has supplied marine archaeologists with a detailed description of an ancient merchantman — shipbuilding techniques, loading capacity,

* Excavated by Prof. Bass between 1961 and 1964.

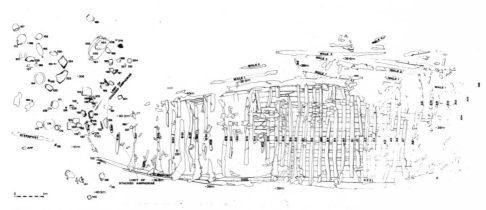

Plan of the Yassi-Ada wreck, mapped by stereophotogrammetry at 140 feet deep

propulsion and anchoring devices, as well as a glimpse of the everyday life of the sailors whose utensils and personal belongings were found intact. The study of the hull by Prof. Frederick van Doorninck, following the most meticulous gathering of every splinter of wood found on the sea bed, has not only presented naval architecture with model reconstructions of a seven-century merchantman, but also expanded our knowledge and experience in dealing with the problems of the preservation of water-logged wood — a primary concern to the marine archaeologist.

3. *Torre Sgarrata*

Once the patterns of excavation, analysis and reconstruction of ship hulls were established, our knowledge of ship-building in antiquity could now be enhanced with every new wreck discovered and studied. Thus the Torre Sgarrata shipwreck found near Taranto in southern Italy, and excavated by Peter Throckmorton in 1967 and 1968, yielded substantial information for our understanding of Roman shipbuilding in imperial times. We learned about the use of various types of wood such as pine, cypress or cedar, the shapes and materials of the nails and the problems of lead-sheeting the lower part of the hull. No less instructive was the cargo carried by this ship, consisting of over 160 tons of marble imported from Asia Minor. Most of it had already been shaped in the form of *sarcophagi* (coffins) — a common item of trade as

Cargo of marble sarcophagi as found, at Torre Sgaratta

attested to by two other wrecks, one found near San Pietro in southern Italy, the other near Methone in the Greek Peloponnese, both explored by Throckmorton.

4. *Marzamemi*

In connection with the marble trade we should mention the cargo of a sixth-century shipwreck discovered at Marzamemi, Sicily, which carried "church marbles". Gerhard Kapitän of Germany, who excavated the site, found scores of architectural elements belonging to a "prefabricated" church which was shipped from a port in the Sea of Marmara to Italy.

5. *Kyrenia*

Following the successful excavations in Turkey and Italy, the Pennsylvania University Museum initiated a survey programme in search of ancient wrecks along the eastern Mediterranean shores. Sophisticated tools were introduced. A two-man research submarine, a proton magnetometer, an underwater television and two types of sonar were put into action. Although some results were achieved and a number of wrecks (mainly in deep waters) were spotted and marked for future investigation, the most important wreck sites still remain the chance discoveries made by fishermen and divers. Such was the case at Kyrenia in Cyprus. A team of archaeologists, led by Prof. M. Katzev, were on the verge of giving up a month-long survey around the island when they were shown a heap of amphorae spotted some time before by a local fisherman less than 2 miles out of Kyrenia harbour. Overgrown with seaweed and protruding slightly from the sandy bottom in 30 metres of water, these jars formed the "crest" of an underwater *tel* (mound) which hid the remains of a fourth-century BC Hellenistic merchant man.

A team of over 40 scientists, students and professional divers directed by Katzev spent thousands of hours on the sea bottom during two full seasons of excavations in 1968 and 1969. The ship and its cargo were found intact and in such an excellent state of preservation, under the protecting layers of sand, that even the shells of the almonds which comprised part of the merchandise were perfectly preserved. The ship carried over 400 amphorae, most of which came from Rhodes, as well as a good number of millstones for commercial use.

A very important contribution to marine archaeology was made by the successful effort of this expedition in hauling up the hull of the ship. More than 50 per cent of its wood (predominantly pine) was found in place. It was a most difficult task, since the wood — saturated and fragile — had to be cut into small sections, labelled and "packed" in containers before being raised to the surface. It later went through a long and most complicated process of conservation treatment. Visitors to the Kyrenia Castle will get a chance, in the near future, to have a close look at the reconstruction of a small merchantman and its cargo which sailed the Mediterranean some 2400 years ago.

6. *Shave-Ziyyon*

A chance discovery made recently by a fisherman turned out to be one of the important marine archaeological finds in the eastern Mediterranean. A number of heavily encrusted tube-shaped artefacts were presented by the man to the Haifa Maritime Museum and, when cleaned, were found to be terracottas of standing females. Some of them carried the "sign of Tanit", the principal deity of Carthage, and thus were identified with her. Upon investigation of the site

Above: Amphorae and grain mills within hull of
Kyrenia wreck

Right: Ancient pottery embedded in the rainbow
of the sea floor

Overleaf left: Divers at work
Overleaf right: Pottery on the sea bed

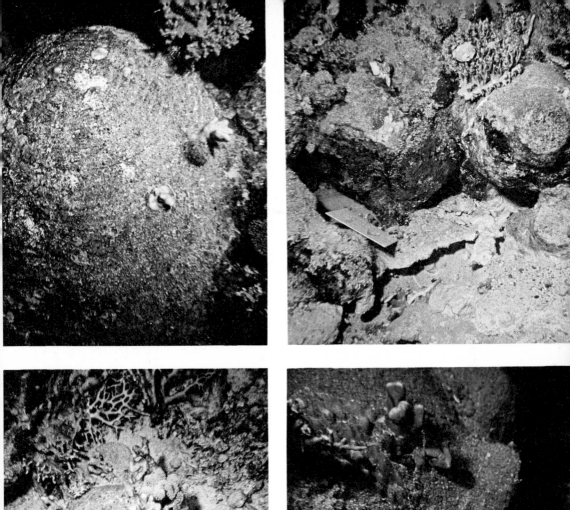

of these finds, located opposite the village of Shave-Ziyyon, north of Acre, it became obvious that a ship carrying a cargo of votive figurines and amphorae had failed to reach its destination, which was probably one of the Phoenician harbours between Acre and Tyre. The expedition, organized by the University of Haifa in conjunction with the Undersea Exploration Society and the Haifa Maritime Museum, scanned an extensive area over which the archaeological relics were scattered, heavily concreted and embedded in the sandstone ridge.

Hundreds of figurines were recovered, forming one of the richest assemblages of terracottas ever found at a single site. The discovery aroused a complex of historical, cultic, iconographic and artistic problems concerning the interrelation between the Phoenician motherland and her colonies during the middle of the first millennium BC. Further investigation of the site and a comparative study of the artefacts with eastern and western material cultures will, it is hoped, answer some of the questions evoked by the ship and her contents.

The provenance of the ship and its cargo has not yet been established. Analysis of the clay used by the potter may serve as a clue. This is now done by a new method, termed the Neutron Activation Analysis, developed by Prof. O. Perlman. It discloses the chemical composition profile of pottery which varies from location to location.

7. *Motya*

Carthaginian maritime expansion and Punic sea power have been the subject of numerous studies based both on the writings of Greek and Roman historians and on archaeological finds at Punic sites. However, material data concerning ships and their cargoes was almost non-existent. It was therefore a fortunate coincidence that concurrently with the discovery of the figurine wreck at Shave-Ziyyon, the hull of a ship identified as Punic, and dating to the 3rd century BC, was found outside the Motya lagoon in Sicily. The site is at present being excavated by a British team headed by Honor Frost. The wreck lies in 3 metres of water and its wood is relatively well preserved since it had been covered with thick layers of sand until its recent exposure. Planking, frames, floor timber, and part of the keel and sternpost were recovered after the first season of excavation in 1971. Traces of calking have been clearly identified and even the carpenter's markings, drawn or painted. The excavators think they may have come across a Punic warship of the type later copied by Carthage's Roman adversaries and put to good use in the first Punic war.

Left: Encrusted amphora on sea bed

Above and right: Terracotta figurines of Tanit recovered off Shave-Ziyyon

If this assumption is verified, the discovery at Motya will open a new chapter in marine archaeology — the study of ancient warships. To date, no ancient warship has been discovered, partly due to their swift disintegration on the sea bed, warships being relatively small and lacking the cargo which normally discloses a merchantman. Thus material evidence of famous sea encounters, such as the naval battle of Salamis between the Persians and Greeks or even the battle of Lepanto, 2000 years later (1571), between the Christian and Turkish fleets, is completely lacking.

8. *Messina*

Not far from the Punic wreck site, in the Straits of Messina, the remnants of a cargo belonging to a fifth- or fourth-century BC merchantman were rescued in 1970 from the hands of greedy looters. While quarrelling amongst themselves the fishermen, who had found the wreck and then pillaged it for months, were identified by the Italian authorities, sentenced and detained. Prof. David Owen of the Pennsylvania University Museum investigated the site with an international team of expert divers. Under hazardous conditions of heavy currents in water over 35 metres deep, the expedition surveyed the site with metal detectors followed by a number of trench excavations. The results were extraordinary, despite the fact that most of this ship's cargo had already been removed by the robbers. The objects recovered by the expedition included various types of amphorae for oil and wine transport and some cylinder-shaped containers of the "Punic type" which probably carried dried fish; a number of leaden anchor components, one weighing over one ton; oil lamps and kitchen ware of black glazed pottery; and parts of at least two life-size bronze statues representing bearded men and belonging to the classical period of Greek sculpture. Even though only small portions of the 25-metre-long ship remained, some details concerning the shipbuilding techniques of the 5th or 4th century were revealed, as for example the fact that even at this early period the lower parts of ships' hulls were protected by thin lead sheets.

b) THE RED SEA

This body of water holds in its depths the secrets of some of the more significant chapters in the history of seafaring. Until very recently the Red Sea was a completely unknown area to the archaeologist. Where, for instance, are the relics of the boats which carried copper ore from the mines in Sinai to Egypt? Smelting sites dating to the Chalcolithic period have been discovered near Timnah, not far from the head of the Gulf of Aqaba. Only recently an Egyptian miners' temple, dedicated to the goddess Hathor, was excavated near by by Prof. B. Rothenberg, proving that intensive mining and trading activities existed in the late Bronze Age and continued until the end of the Byzantine period.

Where is the material evidence for Red Sea trade in the direction of Ophir, where Hiram and Solomon obtained their gold? What is left of the fleet of King Jehoshafat which was wrecked near Etzion-Geber on its maiden voyage?

The rocky, indented western coastline

Peculiar Punic pottery from the Messina wreck

of the Gulf of Aqaba presents many hazards to shipping and so the likelihood of finding wrecks and the advantages of diving in clear, warm water have attracted the attention of marine archaeologists during recent years.

Experience shows, however, that as far as ancient wrecks are concerned, there is a severe drawback to archaeological work in this area, due to the rapid growth of coral deposits (see Chapter III). Thus, at Jezirat Fara'un (see Chapters VI and VII) Prof. H. Edgerton carried out a sub-bottom profiling survey which located medieval pottery under 2.5 metres of sediment at a depth of 18 metres. One cannot be certain that conditions are the same everywhere, but it seems likely that the seabed of Solomon's time lies below 8 or 9 metres of sand and coral layers.

1. *Sharm-el-Sheikh I*

In the shallow bay of Sharm-el-Sheikh, where periodic currents of muddy water from the shore retard the growth of coral, it was easy to locate and excavate a well preserved eighteenth-century ship. In 1968, two divers observed numerous fragments of pottery which stood out conspicuously against the white sand. The Undersea Exploration Society organized an expedition in the spring of 1969 and in less than 6 weeks a salvage operation was carried out. As a result, almost the entire lower hull of the ship, measuring some 50 metres long and 13 metres wide, was exposed and its cargo hauled up.

All the signs indicated that the ship had foundered as a result of fire which destroyed the superstructure and was extinguished only after the seawater flowed into the hold, whereupon the vessel sank. It would appear that the crew succeeded in reaching the shore, taking with them their personal belongings and valuables, since no small finds were discovered.

One thousand clay vessels constituted the major portion of the ship's cargo. The majority of these are flasks without handles. They are unglazed and are decorated on the exterior with a combination of incised geometric patterns and moulded decoration. Each has a

At work on a wreck-site

clay sieve at the base of the neck, and many have lids of a shape resembling a "Tartar hat", some with holes to serve as sieves. About twenty pipe-bowls of the so-called "turkish" type were also found in the wreck.

The pottery found in this shipwreck represents an extraordinary group, hitherto unknown. Various influences can be noted, mainly Turkish and South Arabian. Pieces of Chinese porcelain found among the cargo help date the wreck to the first half of the 18th century.

Thus the discovery can be considered as an important contribution to our knowledge of the material culture of the Red Sea basin during the Ottoman period including a large selection of vessels which have no parallel among land excavations.

2. *Sharm-el-Sheikh II — The Mercury Carrier*

In the summer of 1970 another shipwreck was discovered 5 kilometres northeast of Sharm-el-Sheikh. Sepp Winkler, a Swiss underwater photographer, spotted a group of huge spherical jars and several bronze bowls hidden in dense coral growth at a depth of 30 metres, just as he was about to ascend from his dive. On his return home, he promptly informed the archaeological authorities in Israel of his find. Since the exact location was not given and only several colour photographs were available, a team from the Undersea Exploration Society had to survey over 10 kilometres of the coral reef until the site was relocated.

To the divers descending upon the wreck site, a very extraordinary sight was revealed: huge jars (later nicknamed the "Ali Baba" type) were scattered over a steep slope at the foot of an exquisite coral reef, together with a variety of bronze utensils which decorated the sea bottom. Before work began, it was decided to make every effort to preserve the natural beauty of the site and avoid any destruction of the coral while carrying out the archaeological investigation.

Upon examining the artefacts, divers were surprised to find small liquid bubbles of a silvery colour on the bottom of several bronze bowls and inside a few glazed jars. Samples of the material carried to the surface proved to be pure metallic mercury. It is interesting to note that a chemical analysis of the bowls showed that they were made of a special bronze alloy which included over 20 % lead (to prevent rapid deterioration expected from its contact with mercury).

From a comparative study of the pottery and other materials found at the site, it appears that the ship was wrecked around 1600 while carrying a cargo of mercury, in all probability to be used as a melting and purifying agent in the gold manufacturing process in Africa or Arabia.

The discovery of these two wrecks along the southern tip of the Sinai Peninsula is of great significance to the study of Arabic and early Turkish seafaring and economy in the Red Sea, since so little is yet known of the subject. Furthermore, the fact that medieval wrecks are to be found at a reasonable depth and relatively well preserved despite natural drawbacks gives hope of finding wrecks from much earlier periods as well. New light will then be shed on the role which the Red Sea played in the history of both biblical Israel and its neighbours, and as an outlet for distant exploratory and commercial voyages far beyond the Arabian Sea and the Indian Ocean.

c) Western Europe and the New World

Marine archaeology has reaped a unique harvest in northern and western Europe. The abundance of great navigable tributaries with mud banks (but without the threat of great floods and erosion found in lower areas) and especially estuaries of great tidal amplitude created remarkable conditions for the preservation of boats and parts of small ships which sank in the mud many years ago.

1. *England*

Thus an amateur archaeologist from Britain, by the name of E. V. Wright, succeeded in discovering the remains of three boats from the Bronze Age (approximately 1500 BC) along the muddy banks of the receding Humber riverbed in Yorkshire. These boats were constructed of wooden strips lashed together. Primitive crafts without keels, they were built in a similar manner to the boats found recently in Jutland, dating to *c.* 300 BC. Whether the Humber craft are representative of northern European naval architecture before the Roman era is hard to say, because up to now they are the only examples of the pre-Roman type found in the British Isles.

Even before this discovery, as the foundations of County Hall near Westminster Bridge in London were being dug in 1910, workers came across part of the hull of a vessel from the Roman period. It was identified as a remnant of a Roman merchantman which, though constructed in northern Europe, was built by the shell-first method prevalent in Mediterranean ship-building.

In 1962, a steam shovel revealed large oak planks while digging foundations on the bank of the Thames at Blackfriars. In this case, researchers employed a combined land-sea excavation technique. The site was set apart from the river bed by divider-barriers, and the shallow water and mud were pumped away with the aid of a dredger so that the final stage of the dig took place on dry land. When the excavation was completed, the site revealed that the wreck was a river-boat from the 2nd century AD, constructed in the northern

European method of "skeleton-first" style (though the planking was carvel-built and not the clinker-built Scandinavian method). Following the study of the Blackfriars ship, it was easier to identify and date the hull of another boat which was exposed in the foundation trenches of a new wing of Guy's Hospital in London, built in 1956. This boat was a flat-bottomed river barge, but from its construction it was possible to learn more about the local tradition of shipwrights which had continued for over two centuries despite the influence of the Roman style of ship-building.

In 1939 another ship find had been uncovered by land excavation methods. While excavating a Saxon burial mound at Sutton Hoo in Suffolk, archaeologists discovered a large deckless hull built in the Baltic style (similar to the Viking boats). Metal vessels, trinkets and jewellery found in the same context helped to date this boat to the 7th century AD (i.e. about 100 to 200 years after the onset of the Saxon migration from Scandinavia to England).

2. Scandinavia

Reconstructing this vessel was comparatively easy since from the end of the last century onwards the remains of 3 ninth-century AD Viking ships (from three burial sites in south Norway at Oseberg and elsewhere) have been assembled; providing a guide to the assembly of the English vessel.

The Vikings had employed actual sea-going construction methods in the building of these three boats as indicated by the mast, oar steering, and other navigational equipment. The discovery of these sailing vessels enabled scientists to reconstruct, accordingly and in finest detail, the structure of these massive, deckless ships which had served the seamen and emigrants of northern Europe in their journeys around the European coast, across the North Sea to Greenland and on to the North American continent.

Yet another important discovery contributing to our knowledge of early northern European shipping was made in the years 1957 to 1959. Ole Crumlin-Petersen, a Danish naval architect, and his colleagues unearthed and investigated five ships which had been purposely sunk a thousand years ago at Skuldelev, at the entrance on the Roskilde Fjord, in order to block access to the Fjord. For two seasons the divers attempted to carry out an underwater dig in water whose maximum depth did not exceed 2 metres. Finally in 1959, upon realizing the limits imposed by the existing available technological means, the team proceeded to construct walls around the site. The water was pumped out and a

Viking hull exposed

land dig was begun. In the process, they unearthed the remains of two warships, two merchant vessels, and a fishing boat, all of which serve us in comparative studies with the Norman invasion ships depicted in the Bayeux Tapestry.

With the improvement of dredging techniques, the number of early northern European river- and sea-going vessels discovered has steadily increased. Among these are the wrecks recovered as a result of the reclamation of the Zuider Zee in Holland.

Undoubtedly though, the epitome of northern shipping research in Europe was the raising, preservation and reconstruction of the *Vasa*. The *Vasa* was built as the flagship of the Swedish Navy, but the ship sank in the first hour of her maiden voyage, in 1628 in Stockholm Bay. The Swedish engineer Anders Franzen spent 3 years locating and examining the ship in water 35 metres deep. Then, in 1960, a government project (the most expensive and comprehensive in the history of underwater archaeology) was organized to raise the ship from the sea.

By using sophisticated methods for floating, the entire body of this vessel (which had been preserved in its entirety) was raised to sea level. The ship was then housed in a structure built especially for it, and became a unique museum.

3. *Florida and the Caribbean*

On the other side of the Atlantic, in the Caribbean, a special branch of marine archaeology has developed over the last decade — the investigation of the remains of the Spanish gold fleet. Documents from the 16th to 18th centuries abound in descriptions and data on the loss of cargoes caused by natural disasters and encounters with pirates while making their way from Central America to their home ports in Spain. The lost cargoes of gold and jewellery, valued at tens of millions of dollars, serve as an attractive lure to lovers of history. The American reader is surely familiar with the story of the gold coins sunk off the Florida beaches. But it is doubtful if everyone is aware of the daily struggle between marine archaeologists and the many aggressive and often violent treasure-hunters and thieves.

Anyone who is aware of the special characteristics of the Caribbean, with its coral reefs and the hurricanes which frequently set its waters churning, can appreciate the objective limitations which almost completely prevent the application here of underwater research techniques developed in the Mediterranean and in northern European waters. The surf and the coral reefs have joined forces with looters to destroy much of the sunken evidence.

The *Vasa* raised and being towed

With this in mind, we can doubly appreciate the efforts of Teddy Tucker and his colleagues of the Smithsonian Institute. Their achievements include the investigation and reconstruction of the *San Antonio,* which sank near the coast of Bermuda in 1621 and the excavation of the Spanish galleon from 1580 whose wreck they discovered in 1966.

Also noteworthy is the work of Edwin Link and Arthur MacKay, who located the Spanish fleet which sank in a hurricane off the coast of Florida in 1733; and the meticulous work carried on for years by Robert Marx, who gathered and classified the historical and geographical data on shipping of this region. Mendel Peterson, of the Smithsonian Institute, laid the foundations of the study of the Spanish ships' armament. Starting with a systematic analysis of various types of bronze and brass guns which were found with wrecks or lying on the coral reefs, he reached a conclusive understanding of naval armament between the 16th and 18th centuries. His counterpart in Great Britain, Sydney Wignall, devoted his efforts towards reconstructing the process of manufacturing different types of guns used by the various European marine powers of this period.

V SUBMERGED·HARBOURS

Marine archaeology encompasses several areas of research; we have already discussed wrecks and their cargoes. We shall now turn to the investigation of another aspect — the harbour.

1. *Early Anchorages*

In early times man made use of the anchorage facilities provided by nature: either mouths of rivers or protected bays. Boats were first built to suit these anchorages. They were small and thus easy to manoeuvre when sailing through winding channels among the Aegean Islands or upstream on a river course.

The fast development of large-scale maritime trade in the Mediterranean and Red Sea required the construction of large sea-going vessels. Egyptian records from the 3rd and the beginning of the 2nd millennium BC tell of ships 60 metres long and 18 metres wide. Maritime texts from Ugarit, situated on the North Syrian coast, dating to the 14th century BC, mention ships over three times the size of those Columbus used in his journey to discover the New World! In order to service such large ships it was necessary to improve the anchorage facilities by extending the protective areas by means of structures reaching into the water. In these artificial architectural complexes, which supplement the natural harbour, the principal places for anchoring are the loading and unloading piers. The transition was gradual, with intermediate stages such as an anchorage protected by a sea wall which closes a bay. The inner harbour of *Jezirat Fara'un* in the Gulf of Eilat serves as a good example. While searching for the location of *Etzion Geber*, the home port of the ancient kingdom of Israel at the time of Solomon, an expedition under the direction of the authors reached this particular granite island, called the Island of the Pharaohs, which is situated 15 kilometres south of Eilat and about 200 metres off the coast of the Sinai Peninsula. Between the still preserved medieval fortress and the southern part of the island lies a shallow pool connected to the sea by a narrow channel. An artificial embankment was built by the ancients to close the natural bay, thus transforming it into an anchorage while deepening its floor. Along its shores they built storerooms, the ruins of which can be clearly seen today. Stratigraphic evidence showed that the earliest stage in the construction of the embankment belongs to the pre-Roman-Byzantine period. Several potsherds, dating to the times of Solomon or even earlier, were found on the site.

If the identification of *Jezirat Fara'un* with *Etzion Geber* is sound, we can regard the excavated and constructed anchorage on the island as the transitional or intermediate stage of harbour construction of the later Phoenician trading-posts in the western Mediterranean. The anchorage at Motya, a small island off Sicily settled by the Phoenicians, is of this type. There, seemingly not later than the 6th century BC, a rectangular base was built measuring 37 by 51 metres (very close to the *Jezirat Fara'un* measurements) and over 2 metres deep, with an artificial channel connecting it with the open sea.

The Phoenician settlements in the west needed sophisticated methods of defence in order to hold their own in the increasing struggle over control of the maritime trade routes, in competition with the Greeks. In Utica and in Punic Carthage the inner harbour, called the *Cothon,* became a naval base for the warships whose task it was both to defend the harbour and to accompany the merchantmen on their trading ventures. In Carthage we find a double anchorage: one in the shape of a ring with a building in its centre which served the naval command. This was the military harbour, which was connected by a short channel to a larger, outer elliptical anchorage serving the local merchant marine. South-east of these anchorages we find an additional feature in the development — a breakwater constructed parallel to the coastline with its inner side serving as a loading pier for foreign ships.

The final stage in the development of harbours, the construction of artificial breakwaters, moles and piers, came about not only because of functional necessities, but also because of specific natural conditions characterizing the Phoenician shores. A good example of this sort of harbour is the one at Sidon.

This harbour, together with its sister port of Tyre on the Lebanese coast, was systematically investigated by A. Poidebard and J. Lauffray in the 1930s, a pioneering work opening the chapter of modern marine archaeological harbour research. Following aerial photographs and using helmet divers, Poidebard succeeded in recording and mapping of the

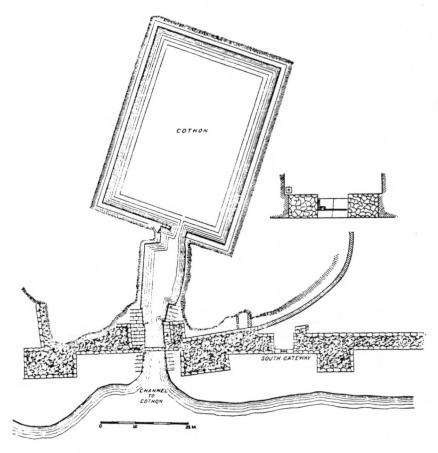

COTHON

SOUTH GATEWAY

CHANNEL
TO
COTHON

0   10   25 M.

The inner harbour at Motya

harbour installations of both Tyre and Sidon, promptly publishing his finds in the most meticulous manner. From it we learned that at Sidon there is a division between the inner harbour and the external anchorage, as well as an additional pier for loading and unloading outside the harbour. The sea side is strengthened by a stone wall which serves as a breakwater, while the side facing the rocky island north of the harbour is built as a pier. Although no definite date has as yet been set for the initial plan of Sidon's harbour, it seems that its division into two sections does not precede Hellenistic times.

Phoenician harbour at Tabat el-Hammam being exposed

2. *Atlit*

A typical example of a Phoenician harbour dating to Persian rule is that of Atlit, on the coast of Israel (at that time, southern Phoenicia), which was surveyed and its installations recorded by the Undersea Exploration Society in 1965 under the direction of the authors. This is a relatively small harbour which served a Phoenician city near by. The construction of the harbour was carried out in one stage and only marginal additions can be detected. The port itself is built in two completely separate architectural compounds, without any land connection between them.

The rich ceramic finds on the floor of the harbour are not later than the beginning of the 4th century BC, and it is likely that this was Aradus — City of the Sidonians — mentioned by the Greek traveller Pseudo-Scylax, in the 5th century BC.

Atlit is a rocky peninsula occupied today by the ruins of the Crusader fortress *Château Pélérins,* which was built by the Templars in the 12th century AD. North of the peninsula are two islets, the nearest of which is connected to the shore by an embankment; its face has been cut and levelled, and it served as the foundation for a rectangular building — perhaps a storeroom or shipyard. A channel over 30 metres wide separates this island from the one further north. Along the eastern side of the island there is a 5-metre-long pier, and from its northern corner a jetty some 130 metres long and 10 metres wide extends eastward, terminating in a massive rectangular tower. The tremendous amount of debris suggests that it originally rose to a considerable height above the water. To the south-east there is a massive gate in traditional Phoenician style through which one reaches a 40-metre-long pier built of long narrow ashlar blocks laid in the "header" pattern, which characterizes Phoenician maritime construction and all the installations of this harbour. From its eastern end another jetty stretches northward about 100 metres into the bay, identical in its plan to the one to the north.

A detailed study of the size of the building stones, the methods of laying the courses, and the relationship between the dimensions of the various architectural components, shows Atlit to represent an advanced stage in Phoenician harbour construction.

3. *Greek Harbours*

While the Phoenicians in both east and west were improving their port facilities, Greek seamen were still struggling with the new demands made on them by their participation in international maritime trade. The rulers of Athens, Syracuse, Samos, and Delos realized the importance of maintaining a fleet of battleships and organizing fleets of merchantmen to make contact with western lands that were rich in silver ore, gold, and tin. Thus it became clear that the larger boats required for their purposes would need deeper water in which to anchor.

The first step was to narrow the entrance to the bay by building an artificial dike which was joined to the fortifications of the city. The lack of technical knowledge concerning how best to build underwater led the people of Delos, for example, to do so by piling up large blocks of stone to make a crude, but massive, sea wall. The Greeks soon learned to add better constructed piers and jetties to the inner side of the sea wall. With the increased political involvement of the Persians in Ionia and the Hellenic peninsula (with constant need for Phoenician shipping) the Greeks became acquainted with Phoenician improvements in maritime construction and hastened to adopt and include them in their harbour installations.

Thus we can see in the harbour of Apollonia, a Greek settlement on the African coast, the stages of development from a roughly constructed sea wall, to the enlarging of the area inside the harbour and the building of a solid structure on which the piers, and even shipyards, were constructed up to its division into a double — internal and external — harbour. A team of British divers under the direction of Dr N. C. Flemming of the Royal Geological Institute surveyed the harbour at Apollonia, and the results of their work proved how much precise information can be gathered from the sea bed, even when one is engaged in the study of such a large architectural complex used during several historical periods.

A similar plan of a harbour based on broad sea walls which were built to narrow the opening of a bay, was discovered by Dr J. Shaw and Prof. R. Scranton during their study of Kenchreai, the harbour town of eastern Corinth. There, changes in the shoreline, which caused the sinking of storerooms and houses in the harbour quarter compelled the archaeologists to use combined methods of land and sea excavation while working simultaneously

in very shallow water, digging through huge amounts of debris at a depth of 5 to 7 metres below sea level. There is no doubt that the results of this excavation, which included discoveries such as mosaic floors made of bits of coloured glass, pieces of furniture, and other rare finds, justified the tremendous effort involved.

4. *Roman Harbours*

With the gradual growth of the Hellenistic cultural *koine* throughout the Mediterranean, it is possible to distinguish three different types of harbour plan: colossal construction — along the eastern shore of the Mediterranean; "plastered" construction techniques — developed in the Italian peninsula (especially in the north, which is rich in material for cement and poor in building stones); the Phoenico-Punic tradition — in Phoenician settlements which became Hellenistic-Roman cities. We shall discuss three harbours, one of each type: *Caesarea* in Israel; *Portus Ostia,* the harbour of Rome; and *Leptis Magna* in Libya.

(a) *Caesarea*

The Hellenistic-style port of Caesarea in Israel was built by Herod, the Jewish king of Edomite origin. Upon pursuing

Aerial view of Apollonia

his ambition to recapture the sources of wealth and trade between the Red Sea and the Mediterranean, from the Nabataeans, Herod re-invested this wealth in the transformation of Judaea from a country of farmers to the epitome of architectural and artistic achievements in the Hellenistic east. Within the framework of this policy, Herod built an international port city to serve as the outlet for his trade with the Mediterranean world and a counterbalance to his capital city Jerusalem, whose people were hostile towards him. Unfortunately earthquakes and tectonic movements have caused the gradual ruin of the remains of this great city whose population numbered, in its heyday, up to a quarter of a million. It seems that the harbour was the first to be stricken by these catastrophes, and most of its remains are now submerged beneath 5 to 10 metres of water. Even so, interest and curiosity in this lost site has never waned, due in no small measure to the description of its construction in the writings of Josephus Flavius, both *Antiquities of the Jews* and *The Jewish War*. In the latter, Josephus wrote:

'He (Herod) noticed on the coast a town called Strato's Tower, in a state of decay, but thanks to its admirable situation capable of benefiting by his generosity. He rebuilt it entirely with limestone and adorned it with a most splendid palace. Nowhere did he show more clearly the liveliness of his imagination. The city lies midway between Dora and Joppa, and hitherto the whole of that shore had been harbourless, so that anyone sailing along the Phoenician coast towards Egypt had to ride the open sea when threatened by the southwest wind; even when this is far from strong, such huge waves are dashed against the rocks that the backwash makes the sea boil up a long way out. But the king by lavish expenditure and unshakable determination won the battle against nature and constructed a harbour bigger than the Piraeus, with further deep roadsteads in its recesses. The site was as awkward as could be, but he wrestled with the difficulties so triumphantly that on his solid fabric the sea could make no impression, while its beauty gave no hint of the obstacles encountered. He first marked out the area for a harbour of the size mentioned, and then lowered into 20 fathoms of water blocks of stone mostly 50 feet long, 9 deep and 10 broad, sometimes even bigger. When the foundations had risen to water level he built above the surface a mole 200 feet wide; half this width was built out to break the force of the waves and so was called the breakwater; the rest supported the encircling stone wall. Along this were spaced massive towers, of which the most conspicuous and most beautiful was called

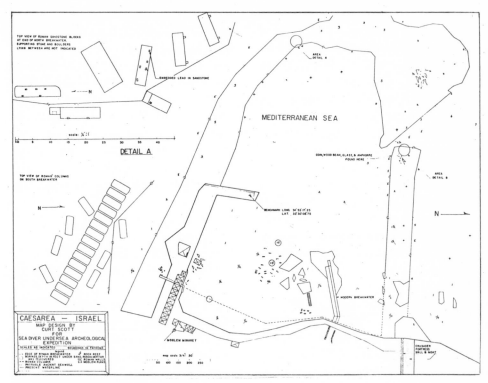

Sketch-map of Herodian harbour at Caesarea

Drusium after Caesar's step-son.

'There was a row of arched recesses where newly arrived crews could land, and in front of these in an unbroken circle was a stone ledge forming a broad walk for those disembarking. The harbour-mouth faced north, as in that locality the north wind is the gentlest, and on either side rose three colossal statues standing on pillars; those on the left of ships entering were supported by a solid tower, those on the right by two upright stones clamped together, even higher than the tower on the other side.'*

A description which is impressive in detail and cannot help but arouse one's curiosity. Moreover, following the excavations at Masada and at the Western Wall in Jerusalem, archaeologists have

* Josephus, *The Jewish War* (trs. Williamson) (Penguin, 1969).

begun to give credence to Josephus' "exaggerated" descriptions with regard to the dimensions of buildings and installations which he saw with his own eyes. Even so, when the divers of the American expedition under Edwin Link tried to map the remains of Caesarea's sunken harbour in 1960, they were surprised at the size of the harbourworks, the precision of his description both of the width of the breakwater and the dimensions of the stones from which it was constructed. This expedition (as well as various surveys which have since taken place) managed only to scratch the surface of what is submerged. It does, however, give us cause to respect and esteem Josephus, as well as Herod's builders.

This harbour was able to meet the demands of international maritime trade; to fulfil the economic aspirations of Herod as the master of flourishing commercial activities; and to meet the growing demand for luxuries from the shores of the Indian Ocean and the Red Sea.

Judging from what has been found, the harbour had two areas of activity: an outer area closed from the south and west by a breakwater and an inner area forming a kind of square basin. The outer area, which also served as a pier, is bow-shaped, 800 metres long and between 40 and 50 metres wide (enclosing an area of about 25 acres).

To the right of the northern entrance to the harbour, two huge square structures measuring about 18 by 18 metres were found. Submerged in 12 metres of water they must have served as the bases for the towers flanking the harbour entrance. To their left, a larger and complex structure can be observed; this seems to have been part of the western end of the northern breakwater though its exact function is yet undetermined.

(b) *Ostia*

During Herod's time, goods from the empire which were transported on the open sea were still unloaded from clumsy merchant ships into small boats that could bypass the muddy shoals of the Tiber delta and travel upstream to the unloading wharves along the river bank. Not until AD 42 did Claudius Caesar dare, despite warning from his professional architects, to budget money and means to build a sheltered harbour in deep water at Ostia, north of the mouth of the Tiber.

The Roman architects used the Phoenico-Punic model in the construction of their harbours; they preferred a narrow, well built sea wall to the gigantic broad embankments of the Hellenistic harbours. Despite the wide area of water in the Claudian harbour, and despite the engineering achievements of the Vitruvian tradition, the installations (not completed until in the days of Nero, AD 54) did not prevent some 200 anchored ships from sinking during a winter storm 8 years later. This even subsequently brought about the construction, in the days of Trajan, of an "inner harbour", dug into the shore behind the Claudian harbour in hexagonal shape. With the completion of this port in 112, after 12 years of work, Rome possessed two harbours, which were connected by canals to the new Tiber estuary, so that small boats could make their way into the city of Rome.

(c) Leptis Magna

True to the Phoenico-Punic tradition, that of a harbour dug into the mouth of a river, to the Hellenistic tradition of using magnificent ashlar blocks, and to the open conditions of the *Pax Romana* harbours, is the port at Leptis Magna in Libya. Leptis, a trading settlement which was previously Punic, was founded in the 6th century BC as one of the three cities of Tripolitania. In the days of the early Caesars it became one of the major ports for the export of wines and grain to ever-hungry Rome. It was therefore necessary to change the existing harbour, which had been dug in the mouth of the river and whose wharves were built of a conglomerate held to-

gether with cement, to a bigger harbour with a larger area of wharves and storerooms. Unlike the harbours previously discussed (except for Ostia) the port of Leptis Magna was buried by alluvial debris, and covered with silt and earth, so that its excavation was done on land.

5. Acre

To round off this chapter, we present a short account of the marine archaeological investigations at Acre on the northern coast of Israel. Its harbour served as a gateway to the East for nearly 4000 years and was used by a variety of people including Phoenicians, Israelites, Persians, Greeks, Arabs and European Crusaders among others. Thus one would expect to find archaeological evidence of the various stages in the Acre harbour construction, representing different styles of architecture and degrees of technological achievements.

Until 1965, modern Acre did not have a sheltered harbour. Fishing boats anchored in the bay with only a row of sandbars separating them from the ravages of the south-eastern winter storms. In 1965 it was decided to built a breakwater which, according to the contractor, "would pass precisely over the ancient foundations, as best we know them..." It was then that we became aware that the architectural remains of this harbour would completely disappear — to be buried under a mass of stones.

Attempts to delay construction work until a budget could be obtained to carry out proper excavations failed; the Undersea Exploration Society was authorized to conduct a speedy investigation while construction progressed. During the months of October and November of 1965, divers worked frantically on the sea bed while their colleagues pleaded with the crane operator to· wait a few hours longer before covering the site with blocks of stone, or at least to hold off until the divers came out of the water! Someone gave the word to the fishermen that if the new installations were not finished before the winter storms, the harbour's construction would be delayed a number of years, which would endanger their business. The fishermen stormed the expedition's headquarters, and took their vengeance by throwing everything that came to hand into the sea. And yet, despite these extremely difficult conditions and despite

Using the air lift

Excavating with the air lift

Starting work with the air lift

the physical danger in continuing the work, the expedition managed to map the ancient breakwater. It was built and rebuilt during three different periods. In the Hellenistic period, to which we believe the earliest phase belongs, several courses of ashlar blocks were laid in the "header" method over a foundation strata of limestone pebbles and sand. Later on, the Romans must have strengthened this seawall by huge stones 12 metres long which were laid across its width. Some thousand years later, the same breakwater was rebuilt by the Crusaders, who employed a method of construction typical of their era—stones which were exposed to the sea were joined together with iron bolts.

Beside the sea wall, and some 100 metres to the east, emerged a polygonal building which revealed several stages of construction changes in its original plan and alterations. The people of Acre call it the Tower of Flies or the Lighthouse. The stratum now at sea-level is built of stones joined together with iron bolts (Crusader style) and is placed on a foundation (now submerged) built of long ashlar blocks which form steps leading down to a depth of 7 metres below sea level. The dimensions and style are reminiscent of the Phoenician construction at Atlit.

An increasing number of harbours have recently been excavated; this has resulted in the fast development of marine archaeology. Among them are Anthedon in Asia Minor, excavated by Dr Blackman of England; Cosa in Italy, excavated by Gen. J. Lewis and Dr A. McCann of the United States; and Aradus on the Phoenician coast, which was surveyed and studied by Honor Frost. The results of Miss Frost's work, published only recently, have substantially enriched our knowledge of early Phoenician harbour constructions.

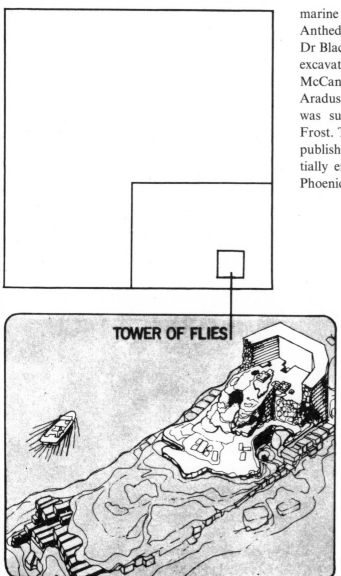

TOWER OF FLIES

Tower of Flies in Acre harbour

VI SUNKEN CITIES

1. *Port Royal*

Port Royal, on the southern coast of Jamaica, was probably the most flourishing West Indian port in the 17th century. The population of over eight thousand embraced almost every profession and creed. Merchants and pirates, clergymen and smugglers lived side by side in extremely crowded conditions. Port Royal's reputation was that of the Sodom of the New World, and the few God-fearing residents of the town fervently believed that the wicked city would suffer the same fate . . .

In June 1692 disaster struck. A terrible earthquake destroyed 90 per cent of the buildings, half of which sank into the sea. The ruins lay in shallow water, then easily accessible to divers. Later on, though, parts of the sunken city became covered by silt; and the covering process was hastened by construction work in the harbour area and by the 1907 earthquake which buried many buildings which until then had remained intact.

Over two hundred and fifty years after the disaster, the first modern-equipped diving expedition was organized, with the purpose of discovering the story of this sunken city.

Headed by Edwin Link, and aided by Mendel Peterson, naval historian from the Smithsonian Institute, the expedition spent one season at the site — enough time to justify expectations as to the potential wealth of information the site contained. This was the first attempt to excavate a sunken city and it proved that, technically, it could be done.

Several years later, the American Robert Marx was asked to proceed further with the investigation. For almost 3 years, Marx worked on the site under difficult and hazardous conditions. In waters of poor visibility, infested by sting-rays, sharks and moray eels, he nevertheless methodically excavated large portions of the sunken city. Many thousands of artefacts were retrieved, including a huge variety of household ware, weapons, coins, tools, pipes and very large collections of pewter ware — all of which served to reconstruct the daily life of Port Royal's citizens in 1692.

The Port Royal discoveries added a new dimension to marine archaeology — the excavation of a sunken city. The results have certainly justified the enormous effort expended by Marx and his team who presented us, through first-hand material evidence, with an almost complete picture of a seventeenth-century harbour town.

2. *Bolsena*

Another submerged site was discovered not in the sea but in Lake Bolsena, some 100 miles north of Rome. In 1965, a civil engineer, A. Fioravanti, discovered archaeological remains in the shallow water along the shore of the lake while surveying the area for the construction of a new road.

Peter Throckmorton headed an American-Italian Expedition and excavated the site for one season. During this short time his team succeeded in uncovering the greater part of a fishing village submerged in 5 to 7 metres and covered by heavy layers of silt and volcanic ash.

Apparently, the village had sunk in the 9th century BC in the wake of some natural catastrophe such as a volcanic eruption or an earthquake. Row upon row of the wooden poles of the houses were found sticking up from the muddy, sulphurous lake bottom. Scattered over the area were thousands of clay vessels and pieces of stoneware — silent witnesses to the once flourishing fishing village.

Until the excavation of this site, little was known of the pre-Etruscan Villanovian culture; the only previous material evidence originating from burial sites in north-west Italy. The pottery types found in Bolsena, some of which were of very highly developed artistic forms, served as comparative material for the study of the pottery ware of this culture.

3. *"Atlantis"*

Few subjects stir the imagination as greatly as the search for the lost continent of Atlantis, an island inhabited by a highly developed people enveloped in a halo of ancient glory which disappeared from the face of the earth. Atlantis left its impact upon the tradition of the Mediterranean people who passed on the story from generation to generation, the border between reality and legend becoming more and more indistinct. We find the most complete account of the tale of Atlantis in Plato's writings where he relates:

> Now in this island of Atlantis there was a great and wonderful empire which had rule over the whole island

and several others and over parts of the continent and furthermore the men of Atlantis had subjected the parts of Libya within the column of Heracles as far as Egypt and of Europe as far as Tyrrhenia.

He then describes the colossal buildings, the three harbours, the many temples dedicated to many gods. He tells of their 1100 ships and 10,000 chariots and relates the catastrophe which led to the destruction of Atlantis:

> But afterwards there occurred violent earthquakes and floods; and in a single day and night of misfortune all your warlike men in a body sank into the earth and the island of Atlantis in like manner disappeared in the depth of the sea.

Nowadays the interest in Atlantis has increased. During the last century scholars and laymen have come up with various theories in their attempts to locate Atlantis — from the North Sea near Heligoland to distant islands in the Atlantic and the Pacific. The dominant theory which remains is that which links the lost continent with the Aegean, correlating the highly developed culture as described by Plato with the Minoan civilization.

The most recent theory points to Thera-Santorini, which, according to geologists, was hit by a tremendous volcanic eruption some 3500 years ago, resulting in the sinking of the entire centre of the island into the sea, thus giving it its present crescent shaps.

One of the major exponents of this theory was James Mavor, a naval engineer who designed the research submarine, the *Alvin,* for the Woodshole Oceanographic Institute. While on a scientific mission in the Aegean, he became fascinated with the stories of Atlantis. After meeting the Greek seismologist A. Galanopoulos, Mavor was convinced that the most plausible identification of the lost continent was Thera and that only scientific proof was needed to confirm it.

After gathering as much information as he could, Mavor recruited several leading specialists to assist him: Prof. H. Edgerton with his seismic profiling equipment; Dr R. Zaruski, a renowned geo-physicist; and Prof. S. Marinatos, Director of the Department of Antiquities in Greece.

Since 1966 intensive investigation of the sea surrounding the island has been carried out by a team of geophysicists headed by J. Mavor and including specialists like Galanopoulos, Edgerton and Zarudski. Simultaneously land excavations have been carried out at various sites on the island. These were directed by Prof. Marinatos and have revealed extraordinary works of art from the 2nd millennium BC.*

Although direct proof concerning Thera's identification with Atlantis has not been found, nevertheless, circumstantial evidence strengthens the possibility that Thera is indeed Atlantis.

* The 1972 excavations yielded several extraordinary frescos; all are in polychrome and are painted in minute detail, and some depict almost twenty ships.

The greatest importance of all these experimental excavations, however, lies far beyond the immediate contribution of a specific archaeological project. The excavations provide concrete proof that submerged cities *are* within the realm of reality; that their remains are there to be recovered; and that legends must at times be regarded more seriously than our sceptical world normally permits.

VII   METHODOLOGY OF A NEW DISCIPLINE

Marine archaeology bases its methods of research on those developed by its big brother, land archaeology, adapting them to its specific needs. We have already touched on the important principle that a number of sciences and disciplines must be combined for underwater study. We are not aware of any other field in the humanities which requires such a broad interdisciplinary base: from geology and geophysics, the sciences which help us determine changes in shoreline and sea level; through the field of biology, which supplies information on the calcareous encrustations that cover underwater finds, and marine engineering, dealing with hydrodynamic laws and the strength of materials covered by water; to the broad spectrum of technological inventions which are used in modern underwater research.

1. Stratigraphy

The first element borrowed from land archaeology is stratigraphy, which is the basis of every systematic archaeological excavation. In our description of the study of sunken ships, we emphasized the trial-and-error methods of those who excavated the wrecks of Albenga, Grand Congloué and the *Titan*. Today, methods have been developed and established for underwater work which permit the marine archaeologist to excavate the site of a ship which is covered by sand or silt, calcareous layers of mineral

Right: Divers

Overleaf left: Above: Divers at work. *Below:* Remaining pottery after surveying and photographing

Overleaf right: Divers at work

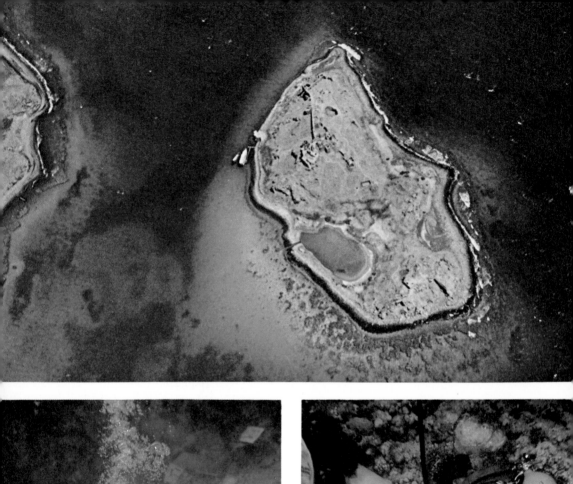

deposits or corals. The excavation can be completely stratigraphical, the only limitation being the water's depth, which of course determines the length of time a diver is able to stay at the site. All that is required is a professional staff, the necessary tools, and a methodical recording of the artefacts, similar to that of land excavations. Difficulties are expected when excavating an architectural complex, whether the remains of submerged land structures or harbour installations originally constructed under water. These, when found in shallow water, are subject to unrecognizable changes. Stones are uprooted and swept great distances away, and massive sea walls, ordinarily able to withstand the forces of nature, are quickly covered with layers of calcareous sediments which completely alter their shape, changing what was once a functional architectural structure to a rock-like mass without line or form. Another problem is that of the typology of marine architecture. The land archaeologist knows the building art and technique which characterize specific places and periods — thus he can draw up a typological system relating to the date and function of the structure under investigation. In the case of harbour installations and underwater constructions comparative material is very poor. The number of reliable reports published on the harbour excava-

tions in the Mediterranean, for example, does not exceed a dozen. The study of stratigraphy and typology of harbour installations and other architectural elements built underwater is at present a major challenge to the marine archaeologist.

2. *Pottery*

Archaeology uses pottery as its basis for dating. Indeed the "science of pottery" has a set of modern criteria which make possible the identification of local ware, as well as the tracing of their import and export, to such an extent that conclusions may be drawn as to the cultural and commercial ties between various civilizations. It would seem that all we need do is adapt these criteria to the clay vessels found in the sea. However, matters are not that simple, as we shall see.

Not long ago a cargo of marine storage jars was found scattered over a wide area on the sea bed north of Acre. The cargo seemed as though it belonged to one single wreck. After close examination, we learned that some of them were "local", that is, Israelite or Phoenician and of a type which is customarily dated to the 7th or 6th centuries BC. Likewise, there were amphorae from the Greek Islands, one belonging to the Knidos Island type (5th century BC), and next

Above: Aerial photograph of Jezirat Fara'un   *Below left:* Preparing a sketch-plan
Left: Below right: Using the air lift

Above: Pottery recovered from the sea off the Israel coast
Left: Stereophotography for mapping the Roman wreck at Yassi-Ada

to it a Rhodian amphora usually dated to the 3rd century BC, together with a Punic potsherd from Carthage. Our first assumption, if following a conventional archaeologist's deduction, would be that we have before us not the cargo of one ship, but remains of a number of cargoes from ships which by chance were wrecked in the same place. However, another approach may be taken; one based on the assumption that storage jars used in marine transport have their own lifespan, and even possess specific shapes which sometimes differ from their

Phoenician store-jars (centre) in Egypt

counterparts used for storage on land. This requires, for dating purposes, a new typological classification of pottery used in marine transport.

A number of attempts have been made at drawing up a corpus of marine storage jars. In 1955, following the discovery of Roman ships off the shores of Italy and France, the French archaeologist Fernand Benoit worked on a new corpus based on the one compiled by Dressel and published in 1899; his work covered particularly Roman amphorae from the 2nd century BC up to the late Imperial period.

Another assemblage is the work of the American archaeologist Virginia Grace, published under the title *Amphorae from Greece and the Greek Islands and the Ancient Wine Trade*. It reflects particularly the collection of containers excavated at the Athens Agora (market-

place and amphorae found at the Acropolis and other sites in Greece. Miss Grace classified the types according to their geographic origins prior to their import between the 5th century BC and the 1st and 2nd centuries AD.

The Spanish archaeologist Ricardo Pascual, like Fernand Benoit, improved and updated the Dressel corpus on the basis of both land and sea finds from Spain and Tangiers. The importance of Pascual's work lies in his classification of the Punic pottery as compared with Roman types. Here the typology takes on a broader regional character, very useful to the marine archaeologist with regard to the western basin of the Mediterranean in the classical period.

3. *Anchors and Ship Nails*

Another method of dating, unique to

Stone anchor from the Bronze Age, bearing incised rudder design, recovered off Atlit

marine archaeology, is based on the typology of anchors. Any difficulty encountered by a ship, whether sailing or anchoring, resulted in the jettisoning of its anchors to free itself or to lighten its load. They are found not only in harbours around temporary anchorages, but all along the coastlines. Made predominantly of materials withstanding the destructive sea elements, anchors are usually far better preserved than any other artefact. Their lifespan is much longer than clay objects, and therefore they are less subject to stylistic changes, which makes for one difficulty in the study of their typology. Despite these limitations there is nevertheless a process of development and improvement of anchors and thus the time and place of each stage can be determined.

In many cases we find stone anchors in a secondary use, which helps to establish their exact date. Builders often incorporated them in walls, used them as slabs for steps and even for votive *stelae*. Such anchors, when discovered in an orderly stratigraphic excavation, give us a date preceding their later function. We have excellent examples from the excavation of the temple in Byblos (dated to the beginning of the 2nd millennium BC); the harbour quarter in Ugarit (14th century BC); the great temple in Kittion, Cyprus (12th and 10th centuries BC) or Tel Shikmona near Haifa (7th century BC). Gradually one learned that the stone anchor with one hole (which is well chiselled) and whose upper part is convex, with a groove for the rope, dates from the 2nd millennium or even the end of the 3rd millennium BC. A similar type, but of triangular shape with a narrow base, belongs to the same period but is found primarily in Egypt (or its cultural sphere of influence). An anchor with three holes — the upper one shaped in a wide rectangle — is typical of the Persian period (6th to 4th centuries BC) and belongs to the Phoenician maritime tradition.

During the Greek and Roman periods, there was a gradual transition from the stone anchor to the prototype of an "admiral" anchor. This type consisted, in the beginning, of a shank and arms of wood and a stock of stone. It changed to a combination of wood and lead, until reaching its final stage, when it was made entirely of iron. Thanks to the abundance of examples discovered in the Mediterranean, it is possible to establish within the framework of this period a reasonable and accurate reconstruction of the lifespan of each transitional stage, and the limits of its chronological and cultural use.

At present two marine archaeologists have dealt with this subject methodically: Honor Frost, who has gradually built up a corpus of stone anchors, and Gerhard Kapitän, who specializes in the typology of lead and iron anchors.

Exposed in shallow waters, the wood of an ancient ship often perishes completely and all that is left of its hull is the nails. A typology of ship nails relating to different periods has not yet been completed. We know that the quality and the form of nails depended primarily on the ship's standard of construction, its size and its planned sailing range. In early times only copper nails were used, but, beginning in the Roman period, many ship builders used iron nails as a cheap substitute for copper. The iron nails, however, disintegrated following oxidation and are of much less value to the marine archaeologist as a dating criterion.

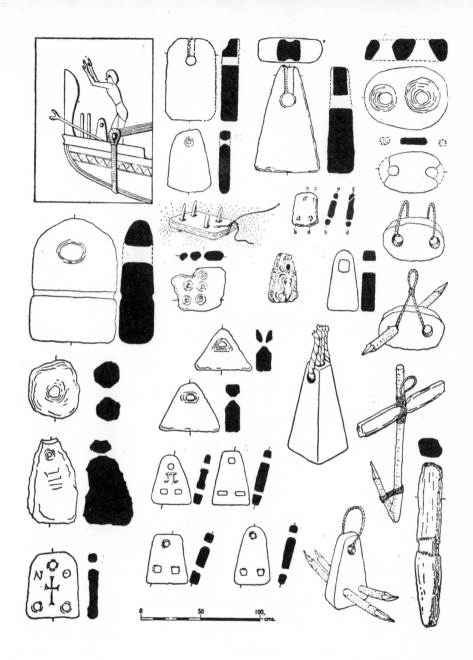

Types of stone anchor in ancient times

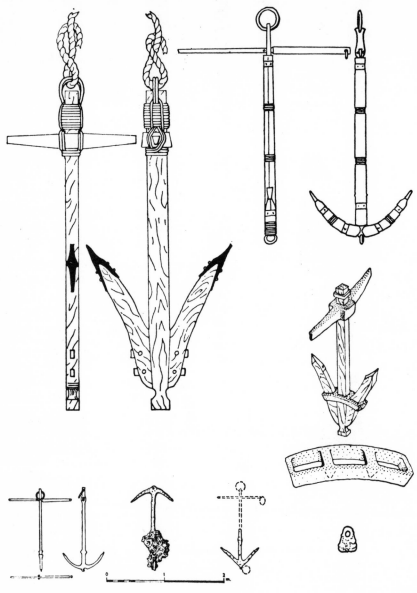

Development of the anchor in Roman times

Small pottery objects such as plates, bowls, small containers, and lamps usually used by the crew often assist in dating a find. Archaeologists are familiar with items of this nature and they can be dated accurately from land excavations of the same type. Arms can be useful in dating ships of later periods, particularly cannon, which remain well preserved under water.

4. *Conclusion*

During the past 5 years divers of the Israel Undersea Exploration Society have been collecting objects scattered over an area more than 4 kilometres long on the sandy coast between Haifa and Atlit. Contemporary development projects along this stretch have caused large areas of the sea bed near the shore, which were covered by sand for hundreds of years, to be temporarily exposed. A large number of objects hidden by the sand for a long period have been discovered. These include pieces of stone anchors; parts of huge bronze statues from the Roman period; Hellenistic, Roman, Arab and Spanish silver and copper coins dating from the 3rd century BC to the 17th century AD; a large number of copper bowls and pots; lead, silver, and gold ingots; a quantity of copper and iron nails; and pieces of metal vessels of all types. To these can be added about a dozen ship's cannon, from the early types of the 15th century to the large bronze ones of the 17th century, which have been preserved on their wooden cradles and iron wheels. It seems that over the centuries some twelve different ships from different periods and various places were wrecked on that shore. Careful study of the distribution of finds however, led us to doubt this, since in many cases a Roman statue lies on top of a hoard of Arab coins from the 15th century AD, and Hellenistic silver coins are mixed with those from Spain under Philip III. Moreover, detailed mapping of the area shows that the mixture is uniform. Despite the accepted view that a sunken ship is usually a homogeneous archaeological unit (dating to one limited period) we have in this case a cargo which represents a merchant ship dealing in scrap metal collected from various ports of call, the contents of which represent casual merchandise from various periods. Such an example can show how incomplete is our knowledge of what to expect to find under the water; and how much more we will have to perfect our methodology to match the requirements of this newborn science.

Submersible decompression chamber at Yassi-Ada

Telephone booth at Yassi-Ada

EPILOGUE

The young discipline of marine archaeology has now come of age and must now face a new challenge — preconceived and planned research concerning the history and archaeology of seafaring. No longer can we depend on chance finds. Nor should we exult over an isolated well preserved artefact hauled up from the depths of the sea. Rather, we should exploit the accumulated experience of the archaeologists, the methods developed and the improved equipment for exploring the sea bottom, towards the solutions of countless problems.

We now possess the equipment for overcoming the problems of limited visibility, depth, sedimentation and encrustation, as well as for the partial preservation of finds. This means we are able to uncover archaeological relics even in areas hitherto beyond the reach of investigation.

The reader has no doubt sensed a disproportionate division among our various chapters. In contrast to the limited material relating to the great maritime civilizations of the past — the Pharaonic sailors, the Minoan seafarers, the sea-minded coastal settlers of Anatolia and Syria and the pre-classical settlers of the Aegean — there is a wealth of evidence from later and better-known cultures of Greece, Rome and Byzantium. This is not due to a lack of data, but rather to the tendency of marine archaeologists to follow up the leads offered by chance finds, to work at convenient sites, to become intrigued by isolated artefacts and to conduct research in those areas where there is intensive diving activity by such people as sponge divers, fishermen and amateur divers, who come across valuable finds by chance.

The time has come to direct our initiative to those areas in which we can expect to find the basic evidence by which to reconstruct the history of the ancient maritime civilizations, whether in the Mediterranean, the Red Sea or elsewhere.

Little has been done in the western hemisphere regarding the search for

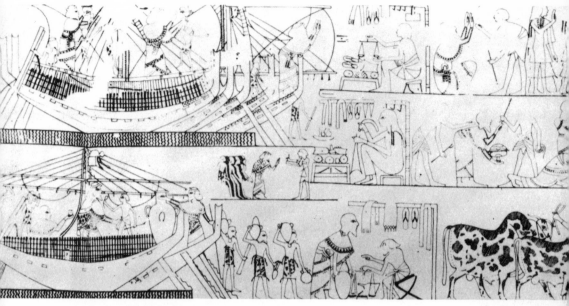

Canaanite vessels unloading cargo in an Egyptian port

maritime history. Underwater exploration in these areas chiefly concentrates on treasure hunting, only seldom diverting some effort to resolving historical enigmas like the routes of the Vikings and their explorations in the new world.

In this day and age, during which the famous Norwegian explorer Thor Heyerdahl sailed the oceans on a raft made of reeds and balsa wood and arrived safely at the American coast; when brave seamen sail dangerous waters in small vessels aided only by currents and winds, thus proving that technically such voyages were feasible in ancient times, we must lead the course of research toward vistas of ancient shipping routes, the technological achievements of ancient seafarers and the inter-continental material and cultural contacts between remote civilizations.

The time is ripe for the gathering of all existing information from oceanographical, geological and geographical, historical and marine archaeological sources; and establishing a "data processing centre" for scientists interested in study and research of the history of maritime civilizations, an inter-disciplinary method of research.

Working under water

Hull of the Roman wreck at Yassi-Ada

ILLUSTRATION SOURCES

Peter Throckmorton P. 8; 9; 25; 26; 31; 33; 34; 78; 86; 87; 90; 91. Under Sea Exploration Society, Israel P. 10; 19–21; 24; 29; 37–40; 45; 61; 64–67; 73–76; 79; 81; 83; 84. National Museum Athens P. 12. Alinari P. 13. Courtesy Kyrenia Ship Excavation: Photo John Veltri P. 36. Haifa University, Centre for Maritime Studies P. 42. David Owen P. 44. Vikingeskibshallen i Roskilde P. 49. The Maritime Museum and the Warship *Vasa* P. 51. From Wittacker P. 55. National Institute. of Oceanography, Wormley, Surrey P. 59. British Museum P. 80; 89.

INDEX